The Art of
Anime
and Manga

Other titles in the *Art Scene* series include:

The Art of Animation
The Art of Comics
The Art of Graffiti
The Art of Graphic Communication
The Art of Tattoo

ART SCENE

The Art of
Anime
and Manga

Tom Streissguth

ReferencePoint
Press®

San Diego, CA

For more information, contact:
ReferencePoint Press, Inc.
PO Box 27779
San Diego, CA 92198
www.ReferencePointPress.com

LIBRARY OF CONGRESS CATALOGING-IN-PUBLICATION DATA

Names: Streissguth, Thomas, 1958– author.
Title: The Art of Anime and Manga/by Tom Streissguth.
Description: San Diego, CA: ReferencePoint Press, Inc., 2020. | Series: Art Scene | Includes bibliographical references and index. | Audience: Grades 9 to 12.
Identifiers: LCCN 2019016227 (print) | LCCN 2019016469 (ebook) | ISBN 9781682825808 (eBook) | ISBN 9781682825792 (hardback)
Subjects: LCSH: Comic books, strips, etc.—Japan—Juvenile literature. | Animated television programs—Japan—Juvenile literature. | Animated films—Japan—Juvenile literature.
Classification: LCC NC1700 (ebook) | LCC NC1700 .S77 2020 (print) | DDC 741.5/952—dc23
LC record available at https://lccn.loc.gov/2019016227

Contents

Introduction

A Weird and Wonderful World

Strange murders are taking place. The victims are robots, and their remains have been found all over the world. But Gesicht is on the case. A skilled detective working for Interpol, he is on a twisting, turning path to solving the mystery. The reader is soon hooked on the surprising plot, colorful characters, and sheer inventiveness of the story.

The story of Gesicht and his robot homicides appears in *Pluto*, a series of small paperback books that appear monthly on newsstands and in bookstores throughout Japan. *Pluto* is just one of thousands of multivolume illustrated stories known as *manga*, meaning "whimsical pictures" in Japanese. Manga and its film version of *anime* have won over a huge global audience since World War II.

Naoki Urasawa, the creator of *Pluto*, uses many themes and visual cues common in the manga art. The hero is a robot, and the story takes place in the future. The emphasis is on constant action, driving the story forward without a lot of wordy conversation or explanation. The drawings are dynamic, using surprising angles, exaggerated motion, and shifting points of view. Each installment of *Pluto* runs about twenty pages, ends with a suspenseful scene, and leaves readers eager to get the next volume to find out what happens next.

Pluto, like many other manga, traces its roots to the work of Osamu Tezuka, considered by many to be the founder of manga. In fact, the author of *Pluto* took many of his plots directly from

Tezuka's most famous work, *Astro Boy*. This series started the craze for manga in 1950s Japan. It was one of the first to be adapted into the animated film and television art form known as anime that followed in the 1960s.

Japanese Art Forms

Manga are illustrated stories that are published in Japan in *zasshi*, or thick magazines that anthologize many ongoing series. Every manga series has a big cast of characters, a long and continuous plot, and a particular drawing style easily recognized by its fans. Small, cramped bookstores dedicated to manga do a brisk business throughout Japan, where people of all ages can be

Stores that sell manga such as Weekly Shonen Jump *do brisk business in Japan. People outside Japan have also discovered the strange and beautiful experience of the unique Japanese art forms known as manga and anime.*

seen intently reading *Weekly Shonen Jump*, *CoroCoro Comic*, *Big Comic Original*, and other magazines. Individual manga series are also collected and published in *tankobon*, small paperback books, with new installments coming out every month. A popular series such as *Naruto*, *Digimon*, *One Piece*, or *Fruits Basket* can run for many years.

Audiences outside Japan have also discovered the strange and beautiful experience of manga and anime. These uniquely Japanese art forms are drawing a loyal and massive worldwide audience and have won the respect of critics of art and film. Bookstore and library shelves around the world carry manga collections, and anime has made it to movie theaters, cable TV, and online streaming services.

Manga and anime have roots in Japan's long tradition of illustrated storytelling. But they have also become cutting-edge art forms that freely experiment with plot, character, setting, production design, and audience participation. Manga and anime creators have developed an amazing range of genres, from office romances to supernatural conflict, science fiction adventure, crime dramas, history, fighting robots, and martial arts. Among the most popular anime series of 2018 were Nakaba Suzuki's *The Seven Deadly Sins*, which follows a group of fighting knights in the Middle Ages; Kohei Horikoshi's *My Hero Academia*, which describes a young boy growing up normally in a world of superheroes; and Yana Toboso's *Black Butler*, a series of supernatural murder mysteries set in England.

Surprise and Delight

Anime is an art that can surprise and delight even the toughest film critics who never took much interest in cartoons. *Princess Mononoke* and other works by Studio Ghibli, a leading Japanese animation studio, had that effect on Roger Ebert, a renowned American film critic, who wrote, "To watch these titles is to understand that animation is not an art form limited to cute little animals and dancing teacups. It releases the imagination so fully that it can enhance any story, and it can show sights that cannot possibly exist in the real world."[1]

Studio Ghibli creations have brought into being a host of odd but engaging characters that include doughy tree spirits, spiderlike bathhouse attendants, wild children raised by wolves, forest gods, and helpful witches. But Ghibli's characters are not out of the ordinary in the anime and manga worlds. Manga and anime creators constantly strive to outdo each other in the wondrous characters they develop and in the inventiveness of the plots and settings of their stories and their art—knowing it is the best way to attract attention from a very big, very selective Japanese and international audience.

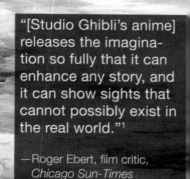

"[Studio Ghibli's anime] releases the imagination so fully that it can enhance any story, and it can show sights that cannot possibly exist in the real world."[1]

—Roger Ebert, film critic, *Chicago Sun-Times*

CHAPTER ONE

Stories in Pictures

In Japan the art of illustrated storytelling goes back centuries. *Emaki* of the twelfth century were long scrolls that revealed a progression of interconnected scenes. Much like the storyboards created by modern anime artists, the ancient tales unwound, scene by scene, through the "pages" of a scroll. The most famous of all *emaki* is *Scrolls of Frolicking Animals*, created by the Buddhist priest Toba Sojo. *Scrolls of Frolicking Animals* was meant to teach religious lessons but also to amuse and entertain its audience. Toba's satirical cartoons depicted other priests as frogs, monkeys, rabbits, and other animals. Modern manga and anime artists are still using his techniques to show running and action and imitating the simple, still landscapes Toba used to pace his stories.

In Toba's time and for centuries afterward, illustrated stories were created for royalty and the wealthy. During the Edo period, which began in the seventeenth century, this art form developed a wider audience. In the 1700s a publisher in the city of Osaka brought out the *Toba Ehon*, a collection of Toba's drawings in the form of a book. An important artist and writer from the Edo period was Santo Kyoden, one of the first authors in Japan to make writing his profession. His *Four Seasons*, created in the 1790s, was the first illustrated work to be described as *man-ga*, or "whimsical pictures." As part of a title, this phrase first appeared in *Manga Hyakujo*, a work by Aikawa Mina that appeared in 1814.

Spirits of the *Ezoshi*

Other popular visual storytelling formats arose in the Edo period. *Ezoshi* were inexpensive picture books, often appearing in series that left loyal readers eagerly waiting for the next volume to appear. Ezoshi were sold in ordinary shops and found a big audience among Japan's prospering middle class.

Ezoshi artists, like the modern *mangaka* (creators of manga and anime), employed many different genres: tales of heroes and legends, horror stories, adventures, and romances. Each genre had its own dedicated artists and found its own audience—readers who, like modern manga fans, loved one drawing style, or one kind of story, and no other.

Ezoshi artists often described traditional Japanese spirits known as *yokai* in their works. The *Picture Book of One Hundred Scary Stories* by Takehara Shunsen, which appeared in 1809, depicted the famous yokai known as the *azuki arai*, a ghostly apparition that takes the form of an old man washing beans in a mountain stream. The *azuki arai* returned in *GeGeGe no Kitaro*, a manga series of the 1960s, and the anime *Kitaro* of 2007. The *shinigami*, a frightening yokai spirit that opens death's door for humans, became a main character in *Death Note*, a suspenseful manga and anime series that drew a worldwide audience in the twenty-first century.

Otherworldly spirits and strange magic were also a feature of the longest ezoshi of all: *Shiranui Tales*, an epic series that began in 1849 and ran for ninety volumes over a span of thirty-seven years. A manga series continuing for many years is now the hallmark of a successful mangaka. *Shiranui Tales* has inspired several of them, including Kaoru Inai, author of the horror series *Shiranui Kitanroku*, published in 2012–2013.

New Stories for a Younger Audience

Ezoshi and other early illustrated stories were created for an adult audience. That changed in the late 1800s and early 1900s. During this era, known as the Meiji period, Japan was forging new contacts with the West and developing its own, Western-style school system. The Japanese government saw the education of children and wider literacy as key to the country's needed modernization. As part of this movement, Japanese publishers brought out the first children's magazines: *Shonen En* (*Child's Garden*), *Shonen Sekai* (*Youth's World*), and *Shojo Kai* (*Girl's Kingdom*).

These magazines had picture stories, or *emonogatari*, that drew on folktales, adventure stories, and depictions of family life.

Supernatural monsters and spirits, known as yokai, populated the inexpensive picture books of the Edo period in Japan. Yokai (such as the one pictured) frightened and thrilled readers of the time.

The stories continued from one week to the next. Instead of the word bubbles found in modern comics, a block of text appearing underneath the pictures carried the story and dialogue. Artists working for the magazines had distinctive styles, and many of their visual elements still appear in modern manga. The big, wide-open eyes of manga characters, for example, date to the work of Junichi Nakahara in *shojo* magazines, which were created for young girls. Nakahara was a doll maker and fashion designer whose illustrations featured large, heavily made-up eyes. Manga artists adopted this look, and big eyes have become standard, especially in those series targeted to the youth market.

Medicine or Art?

Osamu Tezuka was among those intrigued by illustrated magazines. Born in Toyonaka, Japan, near Osaka, he entered medical school in 1945. After many years of hard study, he earned his degree and a medical license. Although the door was open to a rewarding career as a doctor, Tezuka also had a talent for drawing comics—a skill that offered a much more uncertain future. Facing a tough decision, he sought guidance from his parents. His mother offered simple advice: "You should work doing the thing you like most of all."[2]

Tezuka followed that advice and abandoned medicine for art. During the late 1940s he created thousands of pages of comics, which he bound by hand into small books. His timing was not great, since Japan's economy was in a shambles after the country's defeat in World War II. The market for self-published comic books barely provided him with a living, but he earned additional money by creating comic strips for local newspapers. While engaged in this work, he was approached by another artist about illustrating a new version of Robert Louis Stevenson's novel *Treasure Island*. The result was the 1947 publication of *New Treasure Island*, which is widely considered to be Tezuka's first published manga.

> "When I opened to the main text, the shock was so great that I almost blacked out. . . . I had never seen such a manga."[3]
>
> —Abiko Moto, mangaka

The lives of many manga artists changed when they picked up a copy of this work and opened to the book's first spread. In his autobiography, *Manga Road*, the mangaka Abiko Moto describes his reaction: "When I opened to the main text, the shock was so great that I almost blacked out. . . . I had never seen such a manga. . . . This was of course just cartoons printed and fixed on paper, but still the car was going at such speed. It was like watching a movie! That's right, this is a movie. It is a movie drawn on paper. No! Wait a minute. It's not a movie after all. Then, what is it!?"[3]

It was a new style of graphic storytelling that pulled the reader forward through continuous action and movement. Instead of a series of square or rectangular panels, with characters appearing as if on a stage, Tezuka set up "cinematic" pages in which panels appear in all sizes—sometimes a full page. He drew characters from all angles, often from a startling perspective, and used bold exclamations and exaggerated expressions. Over the years, the opening spread of *New Treasure Island* became a visual touchstone for Japanese mangaka. Their goal and ideal up to the present day has been to convincingly depict action in the style of Tezuka and to create a strong and emotional connection with the reader.

Inspiration from Abroad

Tezuka worked hard at his art, drawing more than one hundred thousand manga pages over his career. Fascinated by the science fiction genre popular on both sides of the Pacific in the 1950s, he created *Mighty Atom*. Known as *Astro Boy* in the West, this series is about an idealistic young android with a wide array of superpowers. Tezuka's trilogy *The Lost World* described a team of scientists who travel to a dinosaur-inhabited planet on a collision course with Earth. *The Lost World*, *Mighty Atom*, and *New Trea-*

sure Island revolutionized the world of comics in Japan, showing that this format could support long-running, complex stories that were plotted like novels.

During this time Tezuka was also finding inspiration in foreign works. Japan's defeat in World War II led to a long occupation by the US military. Paper shortages drastically cut the supply of books, magazines, and newspapers. But American troops brought their own comics, including *Daffy Duck*, *Superman*, and *Popeye*. Many of these cheap newsprint comic books were copied and translated for the local audience.

It was around this time that Japanese audiences also got their first exposure to the feature-length films of Walt Disney. Japanese publishers and movie distributors discovered that people were eager for images of a world free of the death and hardship that surrounded them. Tezuka was among those who found escape in these forms of entertainment. "Around 1945, daily life might have been hard, but the reputation of Disney was at its highest," he once told an interviewer. "It really was like the brightness of a rising sun."[4]

Osamu Tezuka's Mighty Atom *(known in the West as* Astro Boy*) revolved around an idealistic young android with a wide array of superpowers. Tezuka's story, which began as manga, later appeared on television as anime.*

Tezuka was fascinated with the ability of Disney artists to give life and depth to simple characters such as a playful mouse, a flying elephant, or seven rowdy, silly dwarves. The 1942 movie *Bambi*, about a small deer growing to adulthood, also intrigued him. Tezuka later recalled that he returned to the movie so often that he lost count of how many times he saw it.

The Manga Magazine

With the success of *Mighty Atom*, life as a cartoonist began to reward Tezuka, who dreamed of the day when he could open his own animation studio. Meanwhile, Tezuka and other manga artists found an outlet for their stories with the introduction of a new type of zasshi, or weekly magazine. "Comic magazines are the first place where manga artists were given a chance to show their work," the Japanese manga critic Haruyuki Nakano observes. "Without them, manga artists would not have been born."[5]

The publisher Kodansha was the first to bring out a manga weekly in 1959. Titled *Weekly Shonen*, it carried installments of several different manga series. Fans read it at home, on the ride to work, and in public everywhere. By 1966 *Weekly Shonen* boasted a circulation of more than 1 million. To keep up

Red Books

In the years after World War II, hardback manga collections were expensive to produce and expensive to buy. For that reason, manga publishers turned to a smaller, cheaper paperback format known as *akabon*, or "red books." These were pocket-sized collections printed in black and white, with red highlights. The akabon cost the equivalent of about ten cents and were widely available in shops, in bookstores, and on the street from book and magazine vendors. The modern Japanese manga began in the akabon, which provided young cartoonists just starting out an outlet for their work.

with the demand, publishers turned to tankobon, monthly collections of several weekly chapters. These small paperbacks were eagerly snatched up by dedicated followers, while bookstores and cafés dedicated to manga reading sprouted all over Japan.

Mangaka who followed Tezuka imitated his now-familiar style. The stories appeared in stark black and white, and characters had exaggerated features, often set at odd angles to lend the scene a sense of dynamic forward movement. Manga panels were smaller than those of American comic books, and their stories seemed to move at a faster rate—the action encouraged quick reading and rapid page turning. A tankobon was designed to be read in a single sitting, over the course of an hour, and leave the reader hungry for the next installment.

The Rise of Anime

Zasshi and tankobon built a mass audience for manga in Japan. Bookstores and cafés dedicated to manga reading appeared in Tokyo and other cities. The most popular manga were adapted to animated films and television shows—a medium known in Japan as anime. Toei Animation, a leading anime studio, broke new ground in 1958 with *The Tale of the White Serpent*, Japan's first feature-length full-color anime.

Toei was well known for giving animation directors free rein in the style and techniques they used. The studio hired leading manga creators, including Osamu Tezuka, to work as artists or to promote their works. Tezuka left Toei in the early 1960s to found his own studio, which he called Mushi. He adapted his most popular manga, *Mighty Atom*, to anime; it began appearing on Japanese television in 1963. Another Tezuka story, *Jungle Emperor Leo*, began running in 1965.

The medium was particularly well suited for science fiction stories. The wide range of special effects made possible by animation made *Mighty Atom* and other science fiction manga stories even more popular as anime. The manga *Mazinger Z* by Go Nagai, for instance, featured fighting robots and their human masters—a genre known as *mecha*. This manga series was adapted to a television anime in 1972 and has since inspired dozens of science fiction movie imitations, including *Transformers* and the super-robot action film *Pacific Rim*.

Marketing and Merchandise

Although he realized a lifelong dream by starting Mushi, Tezuka soon discovered that running an animation studio was a tough business endeavor. Manga magazines were cheap to produce, but the opposite was true of anime, and in the 1960s there was only one way to do it: by drawing a series of pictures on celluloid panels, or cels, and then photographing them in sequence.

The work required skilled artists as well as directors, film technicians, and production assistants. It was a complex, labor-intensive, expensive way to make movies. An animated feature film running at 24 frames per second, for example, required about 125,000 hand-drawn cels. To cut costs, Japanese anime studios reduced the frame rate and used still pictures to save on the time needed to animate movement and action.

To reach profitability, they also came up with licensing. The idea behind licensing is simple—if the show does not make money, then related products will. This gave Mushi, Toei, and other Japanese studios a chance to recover their costs by leasing their most popular characters to the makers of toys, clothing, food, and other products. Offered only low fees by the Fuji Television Network for the right to show *Mighty Atom*, for example, Tezuka agreed to license the show's hero to Meiji Seika, a chocolate company, to display on its products. Merchandising the most popular anime and manga franchises has since become a key element of the manga and anime industries, with related products often bringing in more revenue than the works they are based on.

New Styles and Genres

Animated films and TV series fed off the popularity of Japan's manga magazines, which flourished while anime was becoming a popular new entertainment medium. By the late 1960s *Weekly Shonen* was selling more than 1 million copies a week. Then the inevitable happened for any successful business: competition. With sales numbers approaching *Weekly Shonen* in a very short time, *Weekly Shonen Jump* targeted older male readers with daring new comics such as Go Nagai's *Shameless School*.

From Pandas to Power Rangers

Japan's first commercial anime studio, Toei Animation, was founded in 1956 during the period of economic recovery that followed the country's defeat in World War II. Right from the start, Toei aimed high. Knowing the Japanese people's affection for Disney cartoons, the company's founders set on a course to overtake their American rival's status as an animation leader. Toei's first feature, called *Hakujaden* (*Panda and the Magic Serpent*), employed the Disney formula of cute animals that sang and danced. Later features were based on Japanese legends and adventure tales; many of the heroes in these stories were accompanied by funny animal companions.

In the early 1990s Toei achieved a hit with the superhero series *Super Sentai*. One *Super Sentai* episode, about ancient, magically endowed warriors evolved from dinosaurs, appeared in the United States as the *Mighty Morphin Power Rangers*. The producer of this show, Saban, was adapting other Japanese television series, including *Digimon* and *Samurai Pizza Cats*, to meet a growing demand for Japanese-inspired entertainment. *Power Rangers* borrowed plots, characters, and costumes directly from Japan, while Saban also licensed show-related products such as comic books, trading cards, and action figures.

Many older Japanese readers had issues with this series about rowdy high schoolers who are into drinking, gambling, and girls way more than study. The magazine was banned in many households and inspired public burnings by outraged parents. The controversy posed no problem for the publishers—instead, it boosted sales.

Shameless School opened the door for manga's ever-widening range of subject matter. In the 1970s samurai story *Lone Wolf and Cub*, that meant graphic depictions of sex and violence. Science fiction and robots kept their popularity, while the new *gekiga* style, originated in the 1950s by Yoshihiro Tatsumi, was conquering the manga world. *Gekiga* stories were definitely not for kids, and the characters depicted were far from cute. Instead, hard-boiled worlds of criminals, detectives, fighters, and prostitutes appeared in all their gritty glory, and the violence was drawn for shock effect.

Although weekly manga magazines were developing new story genres, the readers remained largely male until the flowering of shojo manga in the 1960s and 1970s. At first, the magazines *Ribbon* and *Shojo Friend* published manga for girls and women—created by men. Then Kodansha and other publishers hit on the idea of accepting stories created by women, for women. The trend encouraged dozens of young female artists who paid less attention to the industry's traditional taboos on drug abuse, homosexuality, and tough family issues such as divorce and incest.

The new shojo artists invented their own visual style, which they found more suited to the stories and emotions they wanted to depict. They banished the stricter lines of traditional panels to create freer (sometimes invisible) boundaries, images that bleed to the edge of the page, and "collages" of characters unwinding across the page like a floating stage. Shojo manga also played with time and point of view; stories often shifted from past to present and from real to dreamed.

Daring Subjects

Early in her career, shojo pioneer Keiko Takemiya was influenced by *shonen* manga. This genre of manga usually has action-filled plots that appeal to a young male audience. Takemiya was especially intrigued by science fiction, which was the inspiration for her manga *Toward the Terra*. But as the popularity of girls' manga increased, she set out in new directions. During the 1970s she was one of the creators of *yaoi* ("boys love") comics that now attract a huge female audience with stories of male friendship, both straight and gay. "In those days everything was opening up," she explained to an interviewer from the BBC. "Freedom was in the air. . . . I wanted to explore and write about love without boundaries, love in different kinds of shapes and forms, whether it was between man, woman, child or an old person."[6]

Takemiya did much more than open a door for other artists, however. Her works lay at the origins of wide-ranging sexual permissiveness in manga art—a trend that still raises strong objections both in and outside of Japan. Critics of manga often warn of the effect of freely depicted violence and sex, while others point out Japan's relatively low crime rate and suggest that manga and anime provide a safety valve for antisocial impulses. "I think Japanese comics in general are a playing out of the subconscious," author and manga scholar Frederik Schodt told the *New York Times*. "Maybe they fill a role similar to dreaming. You work out your stress, explore fantasies, and then you go back to work and normal life."[7]

"I wanted to explore and write about love without boundaries, love in different kinds of shapes and forms."[6]

—Keiko Takemiya, shojo pioneer

"I think Japanese comics in general are a playing out of the subconscious. . . . You work out your stress, explore fantasies, and then you go back to work and normal life."[7]

—Frederik Schodt, author and manga scholar

21

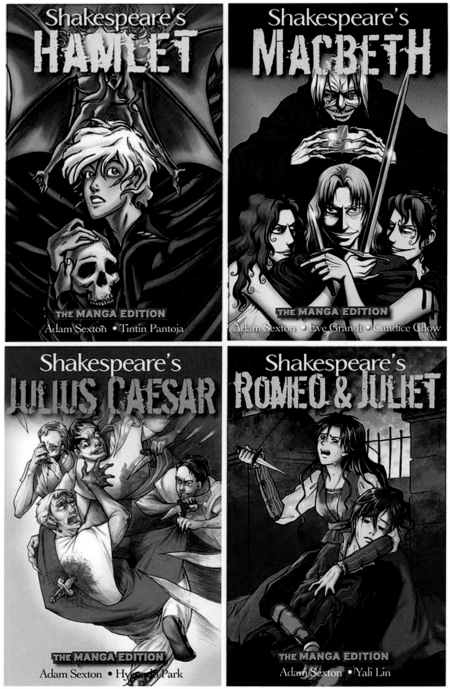

Artists and storytellers worldwide have adopted manga styles and techniques. Classical works, including some of William Shakespeare's most famous plays, have also been adapted as manga.

Despite the controversy of manga's wide-ranging subject matter, the drawing styles used by mangaka have been adopted by graphic artists and storytellers around the world. Novels and short stories outside of Japan have appeared as illustrated texts, and there have been manga adaptations of textbooks, Shakespeare's plays, and the Bible. And manga's sister art of anime has become a global art as well, appearing in cinemas, on Internet platforms, and on televised streaming services playing to an audience of billions. There seems to be no story that cannot be depicted by these arts—and no audience that it will ignore.

CHAPTER TWO

Major Manga and Anime Artists

Manga and anime have emerged as serious and popular art forms in Japan and around the globe. These arts have inspired several major talents whose body of work stands out for its rich, compelling, and timeless stories and illustrations.

Spirits of Hayao Miyazaki

In the feature-length animated film *Spirited Away*, an unhappy girl named Chihiro travels with her parents to a dreaded new home in the countryside. On the way there the family discovers an amusement park. It is an eerie, abandoned place, inhabited by spirits, ghosts, witches, and other supernatural beings. While exploring this nightmarish realm, Chihiro discovers that a magic spell has transformed her parents into greedy, grotesquely grunting hogs. The suspense grows as she plots to save her parents and escape, but the audience begins to suspect that, as in many Japanese anime and manga, there may be no happy ending.

Spirited Away drew huge audiences around the world. It also turned director Hayao Miyazaki into a global star of Japanese culture and film. Born in 1941 as the son of a business executive, Miyazaki took a strong interest in film as a teenager after seeing *Panda and the Magic Serpent*. Based on a Chinese legend, this story about a white snake that transforms into a young woman inspired Miyazaki with its use of folktales, magic, and startling imagery and color. While studying economics in college, Miyazaki also took an interest in children's literature and manga aimed at a younger audience. After graduating, he gave up a future career in business to join Toei, the biggest animation studio in Japan and Asia. At Toei he learned the art of drawing animated characters on film and worked on several different television series. He then partnered with Isao Takahata to start Studio Ghibli.

In a very short time, Studio Ghibli became Japan's most successful anime studio. It attracted the best directors in the industry, who realized their visions with the help of talented artists, sound engineers, and animators. While at Ghibli, Miyazaki himself produced a string of hits, including *My Neighbor Totoro*, *Princess Mononoke*, and *Kiki's Delivery Service*. He was famous for using animation to express views on technology, environmental issues, and war. In *Nausicaä of the Valley of the Wind*, a young princess struggles to prevent further conflict after an environmental apocalypse has left very few humans alive. In *Castle in the Sky*, Studio Ghibli's first production, a young pair takes flight to explore the secrets of a sky-bound castle, while fighting adults obsessed with weapons of mass destruction.

Miyazaki has strong opinions on many subjects, especially on the animation industry. Above all, he does not appreciate the concept of *otaku*—a person who suffers from a total obsession with manga and who prefers characters drawn in tankobon, or a televised anime series, to real life and real people. The sense of art closed off from real life does not appeal to Miyazaki, who once observed that "almost all Japanese animation is produced with hardly any basis taken from observing real people, you know. It's produced by humans who can't stand looking at other humans. . . . And that's why the industry is full of *otaku*."[8]

Miyazaki has always resisted computer-generated, or CG, animation, which is taking over Japan's anime industry. He took

The celebrated anime artist and director Hayao Miyazaki has influenced many animators over the years. A scene from his award-winning film Spirited Away *shows* the elegant, hand-drawn style of anime that has captivated viewers worldwide.

great pride in the hard work of hand-drawn animation, which he saw as a more accurate way to represent nature and life. When a young Studio Ghibli producer showed him a clip of animation created by computer software, Miyazaki did not hold back: "Whoever creates this stuff has no idea what pain is whatsoever. I am utterly disgusted. If you really want to make creepy stuff you can go ahead and do it. [But] I would never wish to incorporate this technology into my work at all."[9]

That does not stop the world's leading animators, in Japan as well as abroad, from taking him as a mentor and admired model for their own work. John Lasseter, the director of the *Toy Story* series for Pixar Animation Studios in the United States, writes, "At Pixar, when we have a problem and we can't seem to solve it, we often take a laser disc of one of Mr. Miyazaki's films and look at a scene in our screening room for a shot of inspiration. And it always works! We come away amazed and inspired."[10]

Eiichiro Oda's Funny Pirates

Working as an assistant in the manga industry can be a real grind. Drawing backgrounds, tracing photocopied images, and filling word balloons until 2:00 a.m. can wear down even the most enthusiastic mangaka. But the dream of creating one's own successful manga has kept many at their desks, including the amazingly prolific Eiichiro Oda.

In 1996 Oda was working for Nobuhiro Watsuki, creator of *Rurouni Kenshin*, the story of a wandering swordsman in nineteenth-century Japan. Recognizing Oda's talent, Watsuki allowed him to create scenes in his own style for the *Rurouni* series. Meanwhile, on his own time, Oda began sketching a story about a young man who roams the seas and continents of an imaginary world. He filled the panels of his manga with frantic physical action and expressive characters.

The young man in Oda's creation, who goes by the name Monkey D. Luffy, is seeking the rare treasure known as One

Piece with the help of his companions, the Straw Hat Crew. Ambition, humor, and the stretchiness he obtained from eating the fruit of the gum gum tree render Luffy and his image quite hilarious. The action only slows down when Oda takes the reader to a backstory, an earlier plot thread meant to explain what is currently happening in the story. In the spirit of pirates sailing the world, the story constantly explores new places, many of them dangerous, supernatural, or simply funny.

Oda has always liked stories about faraway places. He was born in 1975 in the town of Kumamoto, on the southern Japanese island of Kyushu. As a boy, he thrilled to the stories of Scandinavian Vikings, who set off from their homelands to stage bloody raids on the coasts of the British Isles and up the rivers of Europe. It was about this time that the idea for *One Piece* came to him, as Oda revealed in *Weekly Shonen Jump*: "When I was in middle school, I decided that I would draw a pirate comic in [*Weekly Shonen*] *Jump*. I'll ignore the atrocities of historic facts and just draw a bunch of jolly pirates. 'Cause hey, it's summer."[11] He began drawing his own manga while still in school and earned second place in the renowned Tezuka Award competition at age seventeen.

"When I was in middle school, I decided that I would draw a pirate comic in [*Weekly Shonen*] *Jump*. I'll ignore the atrocities of historic facts and just draw a bunch of jolly pirates. 'Cause hey, it's summer."[11]

—Eiichiro Oda, mangaka

Oda introduced the roaming pirate Monkey D. Luffy in a one-shot (single-volume) story, *Romance Dawn*. This became the first volume of *One Piece*, which then became the most popular manga series in history. The series has inspired dedicated shops, restaurants, and the Tokyo One Piece Tower, an indoor theme park where visitors are guided through the games and attractions by characters from the manga.

The first *One Piece* tankobon appeared in December 1997, and since then the books have sold more than 450 million copies worldwide. With the help of his assistants, Oda has been submitting chapters to *Weekly Shonen Jump* for more than twenty years. As of May 2019 Oda had completed 92 book volumes with 938 chapters. Fans are beginning to wonder if the series will ever conclude, and Oda is famous for teasing his readers on this point. "If the time for *One Piece* to end comes," he told an interviewer in 2018, "I don't want to hear the editorial department say, 'Please continue doing it longer.' My ending is as I please . . . [but] there's more story to come."[12]

Hiromu Arakawa Turns Manga into Gold

In the imaginary world of Amestris, the setting for the popular manga *Fullmetal Alchemist*, the brothers Edward and Alphonse Elric are on a mission to revive their late mother through alchemy. In medieval times alchemy involved efforts to convert base metals into gold. The term can also refer to a seemingly magical process of transformation. But in *Fullmetal Alchemist* this art of transformation is very dangerous—a skill to be exercised only by specialists. The brothers roam the country to uncover alchemical secrets, ever mindful of the law of equivalent exchange: anything gained must be offset with a loss.

Fullmetal Alchemist is the work of Hiromu Arakawa. Born in 1973, she was raised in a family of dairy farmers on Japan's northernmost island, Hokkaido. From a young age, she showed a talent for drawing and an ambition to become a mangaka. After high school, while still living with her family, she created *dojinshi*, self-published manga that borrow plots and characters from established series. But to succeed in the manga industry, there was only one place to go. After promising her family not to return until she succeeded in her chosen profession, she moved to Tokyo, where she landed her first job as an assistant to Hiroyuki Eto, creator of *Magical Circle Guru Guru*.

Successful manga artists such as Eto hire assistants to perform routine work—drawing backgrounds, inking dialogue and

Fullmetal Alchemist is the work of Hiromu Arakawa, whose manga ran for nine years and filled twenty-seven books. Her artistry mixed humor, suspense, and supernatural elements to create a compelling and long-lasting story.

text, and composing pages. Ambitious mangaka draw on the skills they learn during this apprenticeship to launch their own works. They also learn to rely on professional connections. In her first published work, *Stray Dog*, Arakawa applied lessons in composition and plotting offered by Eto, who also introduced her to the magazine's publisher, Enix.

Stray Dog was the story of a bandit warrior who takes in a "military dog"—a being with the intelligence of a human and the loyalty and fighting ability of a canine. The pair encounter bounty hunters and other military dogs and venture to the laboratory where these strange creatures were created by an evil scientist. *Stray Dog* won first prize at the 21st Century Shonen Gangan awards in 1999, and then appeared in Enix's *Monthly Shonen Gangan* magazine. The publisher then agreed to run the first installments of *Fullmetal Alchemist*, which borrowed the theme of magical transformation and other ideas from *Stray Dog*.

In *Fullmetal Alchemist* the alchemical arts, with their dangers and endless possibilities, gave Arakawa enough story ideas, plot twists, and characters for a long run of nine years, 108 chapters, and 27 books. For readers, the fascination lay in the way its creator mixed humor, suspense, and supernatural elements to create a compelling story and gave her heroes troubles and weakness that made them seem relatable and human.

Arakawa also kept her story moving along at a fast pace. Her panels caught the eye with exaggerated movements and expressions, sudden and startling events, and familiar exclamations such as *gucha* (crush!) *jabon* (splash!) or *suka* (whoosh!). The audience was also drawn by the heroes' distinct and vivid personalities: Edward's stubborn, rebellious independence and Alphonse's gentler, more passive style—a strange contrast to the fearsome suit of armor that disguises him.

Over the years, *Fullmetal Alchemist* drew a huge audience and sales numbers unknown to all but a few manga artists—quite a feat for a first series. The adventures of Edward and Alphonse were adapted to two television series, two movies, and video games on PlayStation 2 and the Game Boy Advance. The story's characters were licensed for card games, figurines, and other collectibles, and the tankobon books sold 70 million copies. In 2017 a live-action film version came out in Japan. There have also been novelizations of the manga and audio dramas.

Arakawa followed up with new manga, entitled *Silver Spoon*, the story of a small-town student who attends an agricultural school but dreams of escaping the life of a dairy farmer. *Silver Spoon* is funny in parts and serious in others. It is a realistic story, with believable characters in everyday situations. Although some had doubts about the appeal of a story about Japanese faming, the manga was licensed for a North American English edition in 2017. "*Silver Spoon* has turned out to be one of the better grounded slice-of-life stories out there," comments reviewer Jordan Richards. "It boasts wonderful and interesting characters, an easy to understand look, a real world subject for newcomers that isn't made dry or dull to read, and a great sense of humor."[13]

Shinichiro Watanabe's Hip-Hop Samurai and Jazzy Space Cowboys

A strange series of images flash across the screen. Fighters wield their *katana* (long swords) against a scrolling background of roosters, fish, and birds, with a hip-hop track underneath. The viewer feels a bit unprepared—this anime could be anything. In the next few minutes, the story of *Samurai Champloo* and its two wisecracking *ronin* (wandering samurai) will combine action with comedy against a beautiful backdrop of medieval cities and mountainous landscapes.

This is the work of Shinichiro Watanabe, one of Japan's leading anime directors. Born in 1965 in Kyoto, he began his career at Sunrise, a big animation studio based in Tokyo. He worked on the production staff for several Sunrise works before taking on his first solo directing project: *Cowboy Bebop*, still hailed as one of the best anime series of all time.

Cowboy Bebop was a smash hit, allowing Watanabe to co-found his own studio, Manglobe, with several other artists from Sunrise. No longer working for a large studio, he drew on his newfound creative freedom to make *Samurai Champloo*.

The title reflected Watanabe's taste for mixing things up. Samurai were medieval warriors who served the emperor of Japan, while *champuru* (meaning "blend") is a word from Okinawa. This island is a place where different cultures mixed and where the language, food, and culture were much freer than in conservative, isolated Japan.

Watanabe is known for marrying catchy music to fast-moving action. His major influences are jazz—heard in *Cowboy Bebop*—and the hip-hop sound and style in *Samurai Champloo*. Fans and critics also love Watanabe's "anachronism stew," the art of mixing different styles of music and art in a single story. As the warriors

The Fighting Business

The martial arts have inspired many manga and anime creators. Single combat, with opponents using a variety of moves and magic, is a common scene in these works. Fighting also lies at the heart of *Dragon Ball*, one of the most popular manga series of all time.

When still a young man, *Dragon Ball*'s creator Akira Toriyama gave up a job designing posters for an advertising company to take up the life of a mangaka. He won a big audience and critical acclaim for *Dr. Slump*, a comedy series about a professor and his sidekick robot. *Dragon Ball*, which he started in 1984, ran for 519 chapters in 42 tankobon volumes, selling over 200 million copies around the world.

Inspired by the martial arts films of Jackie Chan, Toriyama created *Dragon Ball* as pure action entertainment for boys. He populated the story with dragons, sorcerers, and all kinds of weird and wonderful beings, including a shape-shifting pig named Oolong. The series has been a major influence on young mangaka in Japan. It has also become a huge global business franchise, as seen in television series, video games, trading cards, movies, toys, and other products that have collectively earned more than $20 billion.

in *Samurai Champloo* wander through medieval Japan, cutting their foes down with skill and flair, their story unfolds to the sound of rap, hip-hop, vinyl scratching, and beatboxing, and its opening titles appear in a graffiti alphabet.

Cowboy Bebop takes place in the late twenty-first century, when earthlings use hyperspace physics to move freely around the solar system. But it is not really a futuristic science fiction story. Instead, *Cowboy Bebop* is more of an old western, in which a Space Police force use the bounty system to pay top guns to

Cowboy Bebop*, by director Shinichiro Watanabe, has been described as one of the best anime series of all time. Watanabe is known for marrying catchy music to fast-moving action. A scene from the 2001 movie is shown.*

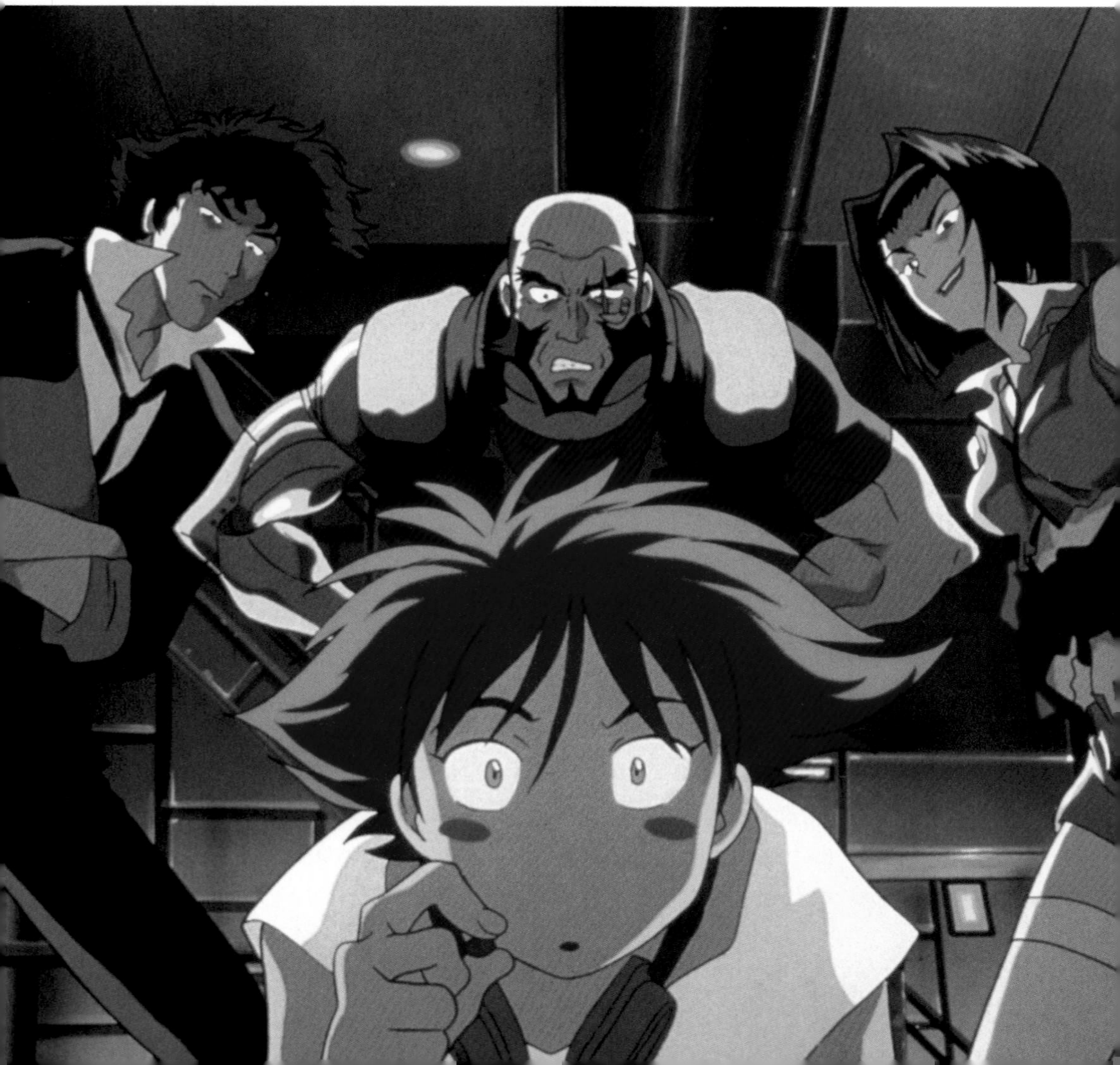

pursue outlaws. Behind it all is that jazzy soundtrack, and in many scenes the characters remain silent and allow the music to tell the story. "[Cowboy] Bebop was definitely the show that you would cite to your friends who thought anime was just 'kids' cartoons,'" writes Maddy Myers, managing editor of the gaming blog *Kotaku*. "I don't know if it worked, but I was constantly using it to try to convince people anime was actually cool."[14]

Cowboy Bebop has been a hit since the 1990s, and many anime fans see it as one of the best series ever produced. In 2019 Netflix announced a live-action *Cowboy Bebop* series, for which the streaming service hired Watanabe as a consultant. In the meantime Watanabe has moved on to the short film *Baby Blue* and the television anime *Kids on the Slope*, a story that takes a familiar anime plot setting—teenagers and high school—and crosses it with a musical milieu of American jazz and blues.

Satoshi Kon, Anime Wizard

Anime creators are famous for not avoiding the harsh realities of life. Many of their films will deny audiences the happy, heartwarming ending common in many Western films. In a sense Satoshi Kon's real life mirrored this aspect of his art. Although his films were few in number, Kon was acclaimed by moviegoers and raved about by critics. By 2010 he was approaching Miyazaki-level status in Japan as a cultural icon, a symbol of the country's talent for surprising and inspiring visual imagery. Then a doctor gave him a diagnosis of cancer and six months to live.

Born in 1963 on Hokkaido, Kon first imagined his future as a painter. But after arriving at Musashino Art University in

Nanase Ohkawa and Clamp

When she was studying to become a professional artist, Nanase Ohkawa took a common path for manga artists. She wrote and illustrated her own stories and made copies at a dojinshi printer—a shop that specializes in self-published manga. Later, Ohkawa formed a cooperative with ten other art students, all of them skilled dojinshi creators. In the late 1980s this group began creating original work and selling it through commercial distributors. Within a few years, several members dropped out, leaving a four-member group that called itself Clamp.

The members of Clamp work together in the same big studio, with each artist working on a single aspect of the manga, such as characters, dialogue, and backgrounds. Although it is a cooperative, Ohkawa is captain of the ship. "I decide who does the characters," she explained to a *New York Times* writer, "and what she's going to do with them, as a director would pick his actors. I assign the roles, depending on the genre of the series: horror, comedy and so forth. I also choose the visual style."

Clamp's biggest hit is *Cardcaptor Sakura*, the story of a girl who allows a mischievous deck of magic cards to escape the book where they are kept. *Cardcaptor Sakura* has sold almost 20 million copies of its twelve-volume tankobon series and has been adapted to two feature films, a seventy-episode anime series, a music CD, ten video games, and three themed restaurants in Tokyo.

Quoted in Charles Solomon, "Four Mothers of Manga Gain American Fans with Expertise in a Variety of Visual Styles," *New York Times*, November 28, 2006. www.nytimes.com.

Tokyo, he began drawing children's manga and reading the novels of Yasutaka Tsutsui, a science fiction writer heavily into virtual worlds and time travel. While Kon was an art student, he also met Katsuhiro Otomo, the author of *Akira*, a manga set in a violent, lawless, postapocalyptic Tokyo. In the anime version, Kon saw how a black-and-white manga could become a work of colorful film art, with new possibilities for action, character, music, and plot.

In 1998 he set out on his own with the feature-length anime *Perfect Blue*. In this story the member of a popular singing group leaves the music industry behind to become an actress. But after being cast in a movie, she finds life becoming crazy and dangerous. An angry stalker pursues her, a killer begins murdering people she knows, and her own manager is going insane.

In *Perfect Blue* Kon created a sense of constantly shifting realities, playing with the flow of time and the identity of characters. "He loved to . . . fool the audience," comments Susan Napier, a well-known scholar of anime and manga. "He would show one thing and then he'll make you realize you aren't seeing what you think you're seeing."[15] The sense of constantly crossing the boundary between the real world and the imagination became a hallmark in Kon's animated features.

After *Perfect Blue*, Kon directed the films *Millennium Actress* and *Tokyo Godfathers*, as well as the television series *Paranoia Agent*. In 2006 he finished work on *Paprika*, based on a novel by Tsutsui. In this story medical researchers use a device known as the DC Mini to view the dreams of their subjects. The device promises some new ways of treating patients for mental problems. It also offers a sinister way to isolate and control them.

The movie's opening credits prepared the audience for the many visual surprises to come. A young woman dances from one dimension to another, springing out of T-shirts, computer monitors, and billboards; snapping her fingers to stop traffic; and creating several different reflections of herself in a mirror. *Paprika* turns life into a dream, where very different logic prevails and strange things happen that make sense, somehow, but cannot be explained.

Critics around the world raved about *Paprika*. Writing in the *New York Times*, Manohla Dargis calls it a "gorgeous riot of future-shock ideas and brightly animated imagery . . . a mind-twisting, eye-tickling wonder."[16] The film made Kon famous not just as an anime director but as a richly talented artist who happened to work in the medium of anime.

But his life took an unexpected turn after he began working on his next feature, *Dreaming Machine*. Diagnosed with terminal cancer, he kept the illness hidden from the public and even from friends and family. "It's so disrespectful to die before one's parents," he wrote in a private statement, "but in the last 10 plus years, I've been able to do what I want as an anime director, achieve my goals, and get some good reviews."[17] Leaving *Dreaming Machine* unfinished, he passed away in 2010 at age forty-six.

CHAPTER THREE

The Scene in Japan

A short walk from the Akihabara train station, in the center of Tokyo, stands the centuries-old Kanda Myojin shrine. People arrive by the thousands every day to pay their respects to the resident deities. They also come to protect their computers—the spirits of Kanda Myojin are said to ward off viruses, malware, and crashes. While strolling around the shrine, visitors leave small *ema* (plaques) with written requests for protection and luck. On many of them can be seen images of Umi, Kotori, Honoka, and several of their friends. But these are not gods or spirits, or even people. They are world-famous idols, recruited by music promoters to sing, dance, and become entertainment stars. As a group, they cavort through the streets of Akihabara in the twenty-six-part anime *Love Live!*

Cosplaying

Akihabara and the Kanda Myojin shrine have become a prime destination for lovers of manga and anime. They stroll through the neighborhood to snap photos of places shown in their favorite *Love Live!* episodes. At special events they can meet the writers, voice actors, and directors. The idol business relies on the good looks and friendly personality of young singers to make a direct connection to audiences, which is also a crucial element for any successful manga or anime series. "I like *Love Live!* this season," said one fan, interviewed by YouTubers in a nearby street. "One of the reasons is that you can actually meet the voice actresses."[18]

Visitors to the centuries-old Kanda Myojin shrine in Tokyo often leave behind small, handwritten requests for protection and luck. Many of these notes refer to popular anime and manga characters rather than to real people.

Authenticity is another key quality. On the popular online forum at MyAnimeList, a fan using the handle 5Cats writes, "WUG [What's Up Girl] is every bit as good as Love Live! LL! and WUG both focus on the characters of the girls and the process behind the idol industry. In both they blend the songs and dancing FLAWLESSLY and both are very high quality."[19]

Manga and anime creators know their characters must be believable, even if they come from the realm of fantasy. If the characters are successful, they can inspire a legion of devoted followers. Some fans even dress the part to show their loyalty to a favorite series. In Akihabara cosplayers arrive in costume, stroll the nearby streets, and pose for selfies with passersby. Visitors can spot Monkey D. Luffy from *One Piece*, Kotori from

Love Live!, and even Pikachu from the huge *Pokémon* series. There are a few Narutos from the manga of the same name, the red-haired Asuka from *Neon Genesis Evangelion*, and even Western imports, including Spider-Man and Harley Quinn.

But cosplay (or costume play) did not originate in Akihabara or Tokyo. In fact, the pastime of dressing up as a favorite character began in the United States, where fans of *Star Trek* were the original cosplayers. In an interview, Japanese writer and anime specialist Hideki Ono told American author Roland Kelts that "we actually learned it from you. America is where otaku started. When I was in junior high, Star Trek fans were the original otaku. They had activities and costumes. Back then, America was already doing it. I never thought it would spread in Japan, too."[20]

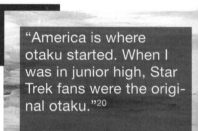

"America is where otaku started. When I was in junior high, Star Trek fans were the original otaku."[20]

—Hideki Ono, Japanese writer

Obsessives

In Japan those who love manga and anime obsessively are known as otaku. At one time, the word meant "fan," then it became a slang term for "nerd." Now it means a person who suffers from a total obsession with manga and who prefers characters drawn in tankobon, or a televised anime series, to real life and real people. Otaku bring their favorite characters from the manga world directly into their lives. They know the stories by heart—they have read the manga or watched the anime many times over. They browse the narrow aisles of Mandarake, the biggest manga and anime store in the world, and other stores all over Japan that cater to their obsession.

Collecting merchandise is a big part of life for the otaku. Fans of *One Piece* crowd into the One Piece Mugiwara store, a shop in Tokyo's Shibuya district that sells merchandise based on Monkey D. Luffy and his pirate adventures. Or they visit Studio Crown, another Akihabara landmark. At Crown, staff will help select costumes, do makeup and hair, and set up photo sessions in a studio decorated as a famous scene from a manga or anime.

The cosplay shops in Akihabara and the otaku stores in Japan offer a wide range of merchandise to manga-obsessed fans. The publishers license their characters to toy makers who make figurines, trading cards, games, and other collectibles. The stories also are used as visual elements in *pachinko* machines, the Japanese version of pinball. For popular series such as *One Piece*, licensing fees and royalties paid by manufacturers account for a bigger portion of revenues than book and magazine sales.

Manga now account for about 25 percent of all published materials in Japan and have a huge influence on modern Japanese pop culture. J-pop and J-rock groups clamor to write the songs for the next anime series, while popular characters appear in magazine ads and on billboards. Japanese publishers are drawing on global fandom as well. An online service known as Otsukai allows otaku all over the world to order manga/anime merchandise directly from Japan.

The manga/anime industry has become a major part of Japanese culture and entertainment. There is no lack of new stories and merchandise to meet the demands of manga otaku in Japan. In fact, the saturation of the market with new works has become a problem. There are so many mangaka at work, and so many magazines, books, and anime episodes available, that overall sales have leveled off. In the case of magazines, sales have declined from 6 million to 2 million a week since the 1990s. Publishers and studios are trying to solve the problem by creating niche genres that appeal to very particular audiences.

Major Manga Genres

Along with expanding their outlets, manga and anime creators try to stay abreast of trends, especially the popularity of different genres. Most fans of manga and anime have their favorite genre, the type of story and characters that keeps them reading, watching, and waiting for the next installment. Catering to these fans,

A Plea for Sales

When sales decline, some artists resort to begging fans to help market their works. Talow Okanishi, creator of the series *Desordre*, went on Twitter to explain, "I regret to announce that due to the extremely low sales of the first volume . . . the manga . . . will be cancelled after the next two chapters. If there is anyone who wishes to see *Desordre* continue to be serialized, can I please ask you to share this tweet and advertise the manga for me?"

Okanishi's plea was successful—at least on Twitter. It was retweeted twenty-one thousand times within a week. But it also caused some pushback, as many fans in Japan were turned off by the indignity of a manga creator asking for help. One of them replied, "You should be ashamed for relying on others for your own gain. If you had time to write this you should have worked harder on your manga." Worse, his series was eventually canceled anyway.

Quoted in Dale Roll, "Japanese Manga Artist Begs Readers to Buy His First Volume, Spurred by Fears of Cancellation," SoraNews24, April 24, 2018. https://soranews24.com.

and creating new and more specialized genres to meet their interests, have become key to the industry's success.

These genres date back to the 1950s and 1960s, when imitations of Superman and Batman appeared in *Weekly Shonen Jump* and other Japanese magazines specializing in shonen manga. These comics targeted an audience of boys and featured heroes, action, and a lot of fighting. One of the top current shonen titles is *One Punch Man*, which features a superhero who can dispatch the most terrifying enemies with a single blow—but is so weary of superheroes in general that he constantly questions his own life and chosen career.

In their heroes, shonen fans look for a strong personality and the will to live. "Ichigo's attitude in *Bleach*," writes one fan of that series' hero, "is more about protecting his friends. He never asked for power, he never asked for fights, he just wanted to live a normal life. But he embraced everything, the battles, the pain, the abnormality of it all, just so he can gain the strength to protect the people he loves. My love for *shonen* series depends greatly on the main character."[21]

As hundreds of new manga and anime were created, the industry developed other important genres. *Seinen* manga, for example, came about as new weekly magazines aimed their manga at older teenagers and young adult men. These stories often include supernatural or horror elements. Some are crime stories that depict rather shocking violence. Others are fantasy series or have sports, historical, or sexual themes. *Akira*, which became a renowned feature-length anime, as well as *Ghost in the Shell* and *Helsing* are among the top seinen manga series.

For young girls, the industry produces shojo manga. There are a lot of romance, fantasy, and friendship stories in shojo manga. The genre features female leading characters as well as idealized male heroes and pop stars. The classic shojo manga is the worldwide smash hit *Sailor Moon*, which has inspired more cosplaying otaku than any other series.

Josei manga are for adult women. They are often about relationships, family, or romance. Some are slice-of-life manga that draw on real-life characters and situations. Other josei manga are themed with action and adventure, with a strong female lead. To appeal to women, they were—at first—designed with covers in shades of pink and purple. Sales of josei manga were mediocre in the beginning. But the genre began to flourish as the movement for women's rights in Japan gained momentum and as manga publishers explored new outlets for marketing their works. "With the rise of social media," explains Megan R on the website Anime Feminist, "they didn't have to rely on traditional advertising or pandering to gender stereotypes through color-coded covers. They could spread the word about new releases directly to their audience through sites like Twitter, Facebook, and so forth."[22]

"With the rise of social media, [publishers] didn't have to rely on traditional advertising or pandering to gender stereotypes."[22]

—Megan R, on the Anime Feminist website

Slice-of-Life and Other Subgenres

As manga grew in popularity, publishers in Japan broadened their market by creating new subgenres. The idea was to develop audiences for manga and anime among people who paid little attention to these arts or had left them behind as adults. There are now dozens of subgenres, from historical to martial arts, military, school, vampire, ghost, sports, *mecha*, and postapocalyptic cyberpunk. Subgenres go in and out of style, with publishers and animation studios constantly striving to catch the latest wave in popular taste.

It seems there is no aspect of life or style of fiction that manga creators have not put to use. One of the hot new trends in the industry is gourmet manga. These stories focus on cooking, kitchens, and the restaurant business—and all of the comedy and drama that is possible around the subject of food. In the 2010s several popular new gourmet series emerged, including *Hell's Kitchen*, *Food Wars*, and *Kitchen Princess*. Kodansha, one of the largest publishers of manga in Japan, joined the trend with *Crocodile Baron*. In this series, novelist Alfardo J. Donson—who also happens to be a crocodile—sets out on a food tour of Japan with his companion, the punky but cuddly Rabbit Boy.

Slice-of-life manga is another popular genre in Japan, one that benefited from the public's weariness with superheroes and the supernatural. Slice-of-life manga revolves around human characters doing ordinary things: working, studying, raising a family, and dealing with normal life issues. There are no robots, space weapons, or vampires involved. But the stories are not always ordinary. One slice-of-life manga with good reviews and a big audience is *Saint Young Men*. On first glance, this series by Hikaru Nakamura about two young bachelors seems like it might be pretty bland. The main characters live in a small apartment in bustling Tokyo, so money is tight, getting around the vast city on the crowded trains is a hassle, and petty tiffs can make things awkward.

But there is a catch: the two young men are named Jesus and Buddha. Having founded major religions with billions of followers, they have a lot to talk about and debate. "WRONG, WRONG, WRONG, WRONG, WRONG," comments one reviewer. "That's what this manga is. Very, very, wrong, but in such a deliciously divisive, amazingly anarchic, furiously funny, and exceptionally entertaining way."[23]

Another major manga genre, known as *meta*, is about making manga. In *Bakuman* two high school friends set out to become manga stars. Their adventures cover the real problems of workers in the industry: long hours, stiff competition, low pay, and self-doubt. Some of the characters are taken from real life as well;

Mandarake (pictured) is the largest manga and anime store in the world. This store in Osaka and other stores like it cater to casual fans as well as otaku, or those who love manga and anime obsessively.

the authors of *Bakuman* base them on people working at *Weekly Shonen Jump* magazine.

As with many successful manga series, *Bakuman* was adapted to an anime television series—a strategy that can turn off the fan base by cutting scenes, characters, or story arcs for the sake of fitting a limited time slot. But for most *Bakuman* fans, the anime worked. "The characters are phenomenal, the overall story is simple, but it leaves you wanting more at the end of every episode . . . a sign of a good anime," comments reviewer Josh Piedra. "You get to experience the highs and lows of trying to make it as a manga author and they try to accomplish this by making it as realistic as possible."[24]

> "The characters are phenomenal, the overall story is simple, but it leaves you wanting more at the end of every episode . . . a sign of a good anime."[24]
>
> —*Bakuman* reviewer Josh Piedra

Opus by Satoshi Kon is a seinen manga of the *meta* type in which an artist named Chikara Nagai finds his own characters taking over the story. When Nagai attempts to kill off Lin, one of the characters in his story, Lin decides to resist by materializing in the real world and stealing the page showing his own death. Chasing Lin back into the story, Nagai finds himself involved in a twisting, turning, and suspenseful story. Kon, a master of clever visual illusion and shifting realities, left *Opus* unfinished at his death, but the story was completed with a final chapter based on Kon's own sketches.

Homemade Manga

Otaku with a talent for writing and drawing have brought fandom to a new level and created another important trend in the industry: the creation of fan fiction by amateurs. In these dojinshi manga, as they are known, fans take the characters of commercial manga or make up new characters of their own and create new versions of a familiar story.

Dojinshi manga artists and authors are like cosplayers. Through their self-published manga, these superfans mean to show their devotion to and knowledge of favorite series, styles, themes, and genres. They mostly borrow from commercial manga, although some also take characters from movies or video games. "When introduced to pop culture media . . . a general consumer will only passively interact with it," writes legal scholar Emily Schendl in an article on dojinshi and copyright law. "Members of the fandom subculture go beyond this passive consumption to make active additions to the media."[25]

The dojinshi manga scene began in the 1970s, when amateur artists in Japan started bringing their pages to copy shops rather than submitting them to commercial publishers. The early editions borrowed heavily from stories, characters, and themes of established manga—and an entire business sector catering to their need for printing and publishing services arose.

At first, this business was small. Bookstores would not sell copies, and word of mouth was the only way to market them. The threat of copyright trouble also loomed large. Earning money from works created by others is a violation of the law in Japan, as it is in most other countries.

Commercial publishers such as Kodansha eventually reached an understanding with dojinshi artists and authors. Publishers agreed not to sue for copyright violations as long as the dojinshi artists and authors agreed to certain conditions. Those conditions include producing very limited editions, providing a source of new talent and ideas, offering valuable market research, and helping keep fan interest in the original work alive.

Tokyo assemblyman Minoru Ogino is known as much for his self-published dojinshi manga as for his work as a politician. In 2018 he brought out *State of the Regional Assemblyman Volume 2—Politics the Yakitori Chef Is Concerned About*. For this manga, he borrowed from the *Touhou Project*, a video game franchise in which supernatural yokai fight it out in the fictional realm of Gensokyo.

To sell his manga, Ogino appears at Tokyo's Comic Market (also known as Comiket), which is the biggest comics conven-

Cosplayers are a frequent sight at Comiket (pictured) and other comic conventions that revolve around anime and manga. This convention is a place for amateur artists to network and promote their work.

tion in the world and is popular enough to be held twice a year. About a half million people show up to this big dojinshi party, which can be as crowded as a rush-hour Tokyo subway car. Why? "Everyone wants stuff that you can't buy commercially," one attendee explained to a reporter. "The things people want, original books—there's a lot of niche stuff. Publishers won't put it out, so if people don't form circles and publish it themselves it won't get made."[26]

Dojinshi manga have become an enormous market, as shown by Comiket's catalogs, which are as thick as a phone book. At Comiket, dojinshi shoppers crowd the booths and tables, paging through thousands of manga reproduced and assembled into inexpensive small books. These homemade manga have become one

Tropes in Manga

Like dedicated scholars, fans of manga and anime love to study and analyze their favorite works. It is not just entertainment to them—it is a universe of different styles, genres, and tropes (expressions that stand for common themes or ideas).

There are hundreds of tropes familiar to the manga audience. "Lampshade hanging" takes place any time a writer points out a strange or unlikely twist in the plot of his or her own story. When a character does not give the expected reaction to a familiar story line, that is "genre blindness." A character who should know better but keeps making the same mistake suffers from "ping-pong naivete."

People working in the industry know the tropes as well, and some even fight against them. Mireko Endo, a young and upcoming anime voice actress, is pushing back against the trope known as "born sexy yesterday," in which young, naive, and innocent girls are depicted in a sexy way. "To be honest," Endo declared in a tweet, "right now I don't know what I should do. I want to be popular. I want to be liked. But to do that, can I really go all the way in acting born sexy yesterday? Can I go so far as to kill the person I am? Somehow, that feels wrong."

Quoted in Casey Baseel, "Aspiring Anime Voice Actress Is Already Fed Up with One of Its Most Common Female Tropes," SoraNews24, October 17, 2018. https://soranews24.com.

of the hottest trends in an industry. Tens of thousands of Japanese dojinshi creators have built their own business model in the shadow of the commercial publishers. In addition to physical books, they are scanning pages and posting them online, as well as creating mobile versions. A common sight in Japan is a pedestrian or subway rider absorbed in a dojinshi or manga page, oblivious to everything but the graphic story unfolding on his or her phone.

The Problem of Abundance

Many of Japan's biggest manga publishers still work according to the traditional model—weekly installments in magazines and collections of several chapters in a series of tankobon. They have been slow to move to the Internet or to pursue foreign editions. This hurts their creators, who miss out on important sources of royalty income.

The industry's low pay does not discourage thousands of young artists who grew up reading manga and who want to produce their own works. There is not much cost to drawing a few chapters and submitting them to a publisher, so manga publishers are flooded with submissions. It is not easy predicting the success of any one creator, as future trends in the popularity of manga genres are hard to guess.

The problem for creators as well as publishers is abundance. There are simply too many manga on the market—supply is high, and demand is flat. Although the most popular manga series command big audiences and major worldwide sales, sales of new magazines and books in Japan have leveled off. Many readers just buy used copies or surf the Internet to get their favorite stories. The advent of amateur manga artists, however, may return the art to its sense of edgy creativity.

CHAPTER FOUR

Manga and Anime Storm the Planet

Manga and anime creators have built a global audience. The wave began in the early 1960s when Japanese anime and tankobon appeared in China, Hong Kong, Taiwan, South Korea, and other Asian markets. Translations began showing up in the United States and Europe in the 1990s. During this decade the futuristic cyberpunk movies *Akira* and *Ghost in the Shell* also set off demand in the Western world for imported anime. Total sales of manga outside Japan now run over 500 million copies a year. Anime earnings—from broadcast rights, movie ticket sales, mobile platforms, DVD sales, and merchandise—reached $6.79 billion outside of Japan in 2016.

Why are manga and anime so popular around the world? One answer is the amazing productivity of these industries. At any time there are hundreds of manga series appearing in weekly magazines and monthly tankobon, covering many different genres and styles. Typical manga bookstores in Tokyo are crammed with thousands of titles packed into display tables, along countertops, and in floor-to-ceiling shelves. By going online, fans around the world have access to all of this and more.

Online subscription services such as Viz Media, Funimation, and Crunchyroll are raising a new generation of manga/anime fanatics. "Crunchyroll pretty much has it all," comments one poster on the site. "Streaming anime, manga, and J-dramas. All legal. Plus, an active message board where you can discuss almost anything, live streams of most conventions they attend, & a store full of anime/manga."[27] The ability to scroll through long lists of interesting stories inspires subscribers to constantly return for more.

Digital editions help manga publishers to extend their worldwide reach. Viz Media and its parent company, Shueisha, have made English-language versions of their *Weekly Shonen Jump* titles available online since 2013. On the company's website, fans outside of Japan can dig into the vault of more than ten thousand past chapters published by Viz and others. And with forty thousand anime episodes available to 2 million subscribers as of 2019, Crunchyroll has broken into the top ten of video streaming services worldwide.

New Genres, New Fans

The range of genres and themes treated by anime and manga are constantly drawing in curious newcomers to the books, anime, and online editions. Many of these new fans have lost interest in hackneyed superheroes that still dominate graphic novels and animated works in the United States and Europe. They are also weary of Hollywood remakes, in which an old original story (*Batman*, *Spider-Man*, *Transformers)* becomes a tiresome, repetitive franchise.

Another advantage manga have over Western franchises like *Superman* is length. While *Superman* has been running since 1938—with many different writers and artists taking the story in different directions—most manga last a few years, hold to a single story line, and then conclude. "[This makes] the art form feel more fresh as newer series take the spotlight off the same old ones," comments one manga fan and blogger. "I've enjoyed my time reading manga series more than American comics because I feel that it is easier to get engrossed in a story that isn't so twisted and long running that even experts have a hard time explaining certain aspects."[28] Also, the vast majority of manga are the product of a single creator's ideas and vision. That means the writing, art, and overall quality are usually more consistent.

The futuristic cyberpunk movies Akira *(pictured) and* Ghost in the Shell *set off demand in the Western world for imported anime. Since that time, manga and anime have developed a huge global following.*

Manga and anime fans are seeking out new stories, as well as themes that appeal to their own experience of life. The problem with traditional comics, in this view, is they are still largely created for and marketed to kids. In Japan and elsewhere, every age, both genders, and all economic classes consume manga. This encourages creators to appeal to audiences that left Western comic books behind long ago.

The range goes way beyond the basic categories of target age and gender. A manga can be a comic, a horror story, a martial arts epic, or a school or work slice-of-life story. New series coming out in English in 2019 included *The Way of the House-husband*, a comedy about a gangster settling down to married life; *Akame ga Kill!*, the story of dedicated assassins fighting for good; *Komi Can't Communicate*, about a withdrawn teenager on a quest to make one hundred friends; and a manga adaptation of a novel and anime entitled *I Want to Eat Your Pancreas*, about young romance and terminal illness.

The anime craze has also inspired imitations in the United States and other Western countries. In 2018 the streaming service Netflix brought out *Castlevania*, an anime-style series based on a video game and produced in the United States. Long before *Castlevania*, the kids' cable network Nickelodeon started the wave with *Avatar: The Last Airbender*, an animated series that ran for three years and won several major awards, including an Emmy for best TV animation in 2007.

Avatar took many of its plot ideas and imagery from anime and the world of Asian martial arts and mysticism. "*The Last Airbender* took its cues from a variety of Asian cultures, primarily China's," comments critic Nicole Clark in *Vice* magazine. "Japanese anime and manga were also a huge source of inspiration. . . . There are also numerous parallels to the art style and philosophical core of the classic films of Hayao Miyazaki, like *Princess Mononoke*."[29]

The Anime Invasion

Led by the global success of Miyazaki's *Spirited Away*, anime has become Japan's most important cultural export—90 percent of the people watching anime on the US-based streaming service Netflix, for example, live outside of Japan. In large part this worldwide success is due to an expanding audience. "These days the anime demographic has widened considerably," explains Tufts University manga/anime scholar Susan Napier in *Wired* magazine. "It still skews young, male 8–35, but there are a lot of older fans, as well as a 50-50 gender split—very different from early days when it was largely male."[30]

Manga producers have drawn on foreign cultures and history to develop new genres that appeal to these new audiences. For the Middle Eastern market, mangaka have created series based on *The Arabian Nights* and other Arab folklore. One of the most popular is Shinobu Ohtaka's *Magi*. "In a sand-swept land of caravans, brigands and adventurers," reads the synopsis of *Magi* on the website Anime-Planet, "legends tell of the ominous dungeon towers that suddenly appeared 14 years ago. It's said that by clearing one of these prisons, you can obtain treasure beyond your wildest dreams."[31] Africa-themed manga also abound. Many of them, such as *Cleopatra* and *Nelson Mandela*, are based on history and historical characters.

The global wave of anime conventions reached the Middle East in the twenty-first century with Anime Expo, a convention taking place on Yas Island in Abu Dhabi. "People in this part of the world absolutely love anime and manga," explains cofounder Arafaat Ali Khan, "and that's mainly because back in the day— I'm talking about the early 1980s—we received tons of original anime series on our televisions."[32] As more imported anime made their way to Middle East television networks, the interest spread among children as well as adults. Abu Dhabi and Dubai, the capital of the United Arab Emirates, have now become hot spots for anime and manga groups, including the Abu Dhabi Anime Club and Anime Manga Cosplay Middle East.

In Europe manga are especially hot in France, proud and ancient home of the *bande dessinée*, or graphic novel. The anime wave began with Japanese-produced series running on French children's television. "People found the cartoons violent and vulgar, with much criticism coming from teachers," explains Cécile

Sakai, director of the French Research Institute on Japan. "Yet this audience was the key to its success, for these children developed a passion for manga and began to buy them in books and translations, sometimes even ending up enrolling in Japanese universities and becoming specialists!"[33]

A Palestinian schoolboy in Nazareth (in Israel) follows the action in his Dragon Ball Z *manga. Anime and manga have won fans among adults and children in some parts of the Middle East.*

By 2019 imported manga had captured almost half the audience for comics and graphic novels in Europe. An important element of the trend is the taste for *kawaii*, or "cuteness" in Japanese. "I realized we are amid a world *kawaii* revolution," writes Takamasa Sakurai in the Tokyo newspaper *Yomiuri Shimbun*, "[when] I heard girls in Europe talking about how they wanted to be Japanese, or that Japanese high school uniforms symbolize freedom."[34] Also revealing of the global fever for Japanese culture are the packed comics conventions that take place throughout the year and all over the world.

The Big Conventions

Crowds of eager manga readers and anime fans rush to the bustling events known as comic cons. At the biggest conventions — in Tokyo, New York, and Los Angeles — it is common to wait at

Do Not Call Them Cartoons

Critic Colin Marshall echoes the opinion of fans of Japanese anime, who have a strong objection to a certain word associated with animation in the West:

> Those who have become interested in Japan in the past twenty years have done so, likely as not, because of Japanese animation, best known by the Japanese term "anime." And why not? Japan's take on the cartoon has at this point evolved so high and so distant from its western counterparts that you sometimes can't help staring, transfixed. Even the word "cartoon" now seems too frivolous to apply.

In the Western world anime lovers do not like to hear the word *cartoon* used to describe their favorite Japanese art form. The debate over terminology does not arise in Japan, where the only word used to describe all animated films and television series is *anime*.

Colin Marshall, "Japanese Cartoons from the 1920s and 30s Reveal the Stylistic Roots of Anime," Open Culture, November 5, 2012. www.openculture.com.

the doors for an hour or two as ticket holders jostle to the front. Although they were once free and open to anybody, most conventions now sell tickets, and many set aside a day or two exclusively for industry insiders and the media.

For ordinary fans, the promised fun and fascination inside make the wait worthwhile. Publishers put their latest editions on display, and cosplayers stroll the aisles. The premieres of new anime have become a big part of these conventions, and many now feature anime in a starring role. More than two hundred anime conventions, in cities large and small, were scheduled in the United States in 2019, under names like Omnicon (in Cookeville, Tennessee) and Kawaii Kon (in Honolulu, Hawaii).

Conventions are a way to boost revenue for publishers selling books or movie tickets, as well as a way to create buzz for new work. Manga and anime creators make appearances to talk with fans and sign autographs. Sponsored by anime production companies, voice actors also show up to mingle with their fans at conventions. Academics and critics attend panel discussions in spaces off the main hall. Experts or creators sit onstage at a long table, discussing trends in the industry or the production of an upcoming movie or TV series.

At the biggest convention of them all, the 2018 Anime Expo, or AX, in Los Angeles, fans jammed the premieres of two new anime series: *JoJo's Bizarre Adventure: Golden Wind* and *Ultraman*. Premieres, pilot (first) shows, and sneak peeks give the producers a chance to gauge audience interest, hear feedback, and reveal new episodes and characters. Anime Expo also promoted the industry globally with AX Livestream, fifty hours of video content streamed around the world via the Internet.

Conventions are all about creative entertainment marketing. For a comic con or anime expo, producers come up with fashion shows, contests, and interactive games to promote their works. For the *JoJo* series at AX, an escape game titled JoJo's Bizarre Escape: The Hotel set up a puzzling maze, with teams of six attendees each navigating through a series of rooms. Fans spent an hour absorbed in the anime's world while interacting with film clips, music, cosplaying characters, and, at the end, a solution walkthrough.

Anime cons also provide a venue for new gear. Futuristic tech holds major interest for these audiences, many of whom were raised on science fiction and robot battles. At the 2018 AX, thousands of fans lined up for *Tales of Wedding Rings*, a seinen manga series about a newlywed couple contending with an evil king in a fantasy world. The audience was wearing headsets to watch a virtual reality (VR) version of the story.

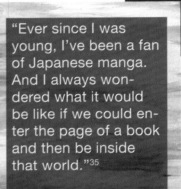

"Ever since I was young, I've been a fan of Japanese manga. And I always wondered what it would be like if we could enter the page of a book and then be inside that world."[35]

—Kaei Sou, virtual reality publisher

In VR the characters move in three dimensions as the scenes shift and the story unfolds around the viewer. "Ever since I was young, I've been a fan of Japanese manga," Kaei Sou of Square Enix, the work's publisher, said in an interview. "And I always wondered what it would be like if we could enter the page of a book and then be inside that world."[35] This new format expands the manga and anime audience to gamers who are moving to new platforms such as Oculus Rift and PlayStation VR. The adoption of VR also helps the industry by associating manga and anime with new, cutting-edge trends in the world of technology and entertainment.

Box Office and Home Entertainment

Conventions may be great for promoting new works, but as a globally popular art form, anime really breaks out when a blockbuster movie garners huge ticket sales, prestigious awards, and flattering media attention. Miyazaki's *Spirited Away* was one of the first global anime megahits. Fifteen years later its box office take was finally surpassed by *Your Name*, which premiered at Anime Expo in 2016. Like many of Makoto Shinkai's films, *Your*

Name combines a science fiction premise with a bittersweet story of growing pains, boredom, alienation, and awkward love.

The anime has earned many rave reviews and almost $400 million in ticket sales around the world, beating out *Spirited Away* for the honor of highest-grossing anime of all time. The film especially appealed to teenagers who—no matter where they lived—could relate to the the dream of escaping to a more exciting place or a different body altogether.

Sheer escapism, for teenagers as well as adults, has always been a big part of the appeal of manga and anime. "I love anime for the same reason I love books and real image series: it entertains me and distracts me from my daily [worryings]," explains Paula Llanguas on the online forum Quora. "Through anime I can experience new stories and live through the characters."[36]

On his blog *Anime Corps*, novelist Tsuyuki comments, "The reasons I've heard western fans . . . got into it was this vast sea of fantasies to get lost in. Fantasy tales that seldom were told in an even remotely similar way in the west."[37]

New Platforms, New Problems

Anime and manga's international appeal has been boosted by new platforms found on mobile phones and the Internet. Online fan sites allow devotees to draw characters, write stories, and chat about their favorite shows. PaigeeWorld, one of the biggest, is a worldwide social network that allows users to submit drawings, enter contests, take art tutorials, and chat via Twitter. Every day, the site logs about fifteen thousand uploads of user artwork, with most originating in North America. "PaigeeWorld is specifically meant for anime/manga which most apps aren't focused on," comments one reviewer on the Apple App Store website. "[It] also has tons of different contests and fun things to participate in, with rewards that encourage people to draw, and get better."[38]

Shueisha, the publisher of *Weekly Shonen Jump* and a big name in the manga world, has created Manga Plus. Fans of *One*

Piece, *My Hero Academia*, *Naruto*, *Tokyo Ghoul*, and other long series can access every installment, in English, on this website, as well as on their mobile phones. Another story appearing across a wide variety of platforms is *Ensemble Stars!*, a story about a private school for boy pop star idols. This series began in 2015 as a CCG (card-collecting game). It was then adapted to novels, manga, anime, and a phone app, in which *Ensemble Stars!* players scout talent at the fictional Yumenosaki Academy to collect promising male idols and train them. As the idols learn new songs and talents, the player earns points, levels up, and collects rewards.

Online streaming services such as Amazon Prime and Netflix have also become major animation producers. Production I.G, Wit Studio, and Studio Bones—all Japanese production houses— signed more than fifty deals in 2018 with Netflix to create new anime, which the platform can bring to audiences in nearly two hundred countries.

This arrangement is not always successful. Netflix offers hundreds of anime series and movies, all competing for the time and attention of viewers. And even when working for a global audience, producers have to deal with changing tastes, tight budgets, and piracy of their work. Kyoto Animation, the Japanese producer of *Violet Evergarden*, has experienced many of these challenges. The original story by Kana Akatsuki appeared as a *ranobe*, or "light novel," a book with illustrations in the manga style. It describes the life and adventures of an auto memory doll, the term for a professional ghostwriter who helps those who want to tell stories or send a love letter but just cannot seem to write.

When it first came out in 2015 in Japan, *Violet Evergarden* won a big audience and several prestigious awards. Netflix then partnered with Kyoto Animation for an anime series. The US company followed its standard model, releasing all of the show's thirteen episodes at once (for binge-watching purposes), except in the United States. The goal was to create buzz and excitement around the world—and then release the show to a big, eagerly waiting American audience.

Chinese cartoonist Xiao Bai is one of a handful of artists from outside Japan who have won the International Manga Award. She won for her comic So Far and So Near.

But things did not go according to plan. Dozens of pirated versions appeared on the Internet at about the same time as the new episodes. Instead of waiting for the whole series to come out at once, American fans just went online. Or they went to a VPN (virtual private network) for "spoofing" purposes, allowing them to watch content already released in another country. Once they had seen the show, American *Violet Evergarden* fans were not too excited when it finally appeared on television in their own country.

And since Netflix pays for the number of views a show gets, the result of disinterested audiences is less income for production houses and their artists. "If most American fans . . . are not excited about a show while it's coming out," explains Lauren Orsini, games critic for *Forbes* magazine, "they're less likely to support the show. . . . When Netflix buys the rights to shows and then holds them hostage, it hurts fans. And when fans in turn pirate the show so they can see the anime they've been waiting for, it hurts creators."[39]

New Artists Abroad

Despite the challenges of marketing and earning from manga and anime, these art forms have attracted many creative artists living outside of Japan. A homegrown French manga industry has produced its own stars, such as Frédéric Boilet. A longtime resident of Japan, Boilet was important in starting the movement known as nouvelle manga, in which artists from Europe and Japan attempt to bridge the cultural divide in graphic novels. Boilet's slice-of-life works are set in Japan and include *Tôkyô Est Mon Jardin* (*Tokyo Is My Garden*) and *Demi-Tour* (*U-turn*), both of which have been translated into Japanese. In 2001 his work *Yukiko's Spinach* was published simultaneously in French and Japanese.

In 2008 Felipe Smith, born and raised in Ohio, became the first Westerner to see his manga (*Peepo Choo*) published in Japan before the work appeared in the United States. *Peepo Choo* is about an otaku from Chicago who goes to Japan to live his dream in the world capital of manga. The Japanese company Kodansha published the story in monthly installments in *Morning 2* magazine.

A Manga's Soccer Glory

Soccer has many wildly popular international stars, such as Lionel Messi, Cristiano Ronaldo, and Neymar. But one towers above them all—Oliver Atom, the megastar of *Súpercampeones* (in Latin America) and *Oliver and Benji* (in Europe). This manga hit by Yoichi Takahashi was adapted to a short-running television version in Japan, then adapted yet again for audiences in Europe, South America, and many other soccer-mad corners of the world.

Takahashi's hero works his way up from a humble high school squad to star of the Japanese national team. He uses all kinds of crazy trick plays—many of them only possible in the pages of a manga or the scenes of an anime. Oliver Atom inspired many players when they were young, including Spain's talented striker Fernando Torres. "I remember when I was a kid," Torres told one reporter. "Everyone in school was talking about this cartoon about soccer from Japan. I started playing soccer because of that."

Oliver is also given credit for boosting the popularity of soccer in Japan, which first qualified for the World Cup in 1998 and now has the best national soccer teams, male and female, in Asia. Takahashi has even claimed that Japan's players were using plays they learned from Oliver when they defeated Colombia in 2018—the first time in history Asians beat South Americans at the World Cup.

Quoted in Wilson Liévano, "*Súpercampeones*: The Anime That Inspired a Generation of Latin American Soccer Greats," Remezcla, July 12, 2018. https://remezcla.com.

The story echoed some events in Smith's own life, including the four years he lived in Japan and worked as a manga illustrator. Raised on American graphic novels and comics, he later found something just as appealing in the manga world. In an interview on the Anime News Network, Smith explains,

Unlike most manga-inspired artists I know, I wasn't so much wowed by the [style of] manga as I was by its incredible abundance of ordinary, lifelike, slice-of-life scenarios and characters. . . . The more I found Japanese comics that interested me, the more I got excited about the possibility of working in an industry that provided material I could be excited about.[40]

After *Peepo Choo* finished, Smith continued to propose ideas for new stories, but publishers turned them all down. He returned to the United States in 2012 and landed the job of storyboarder and character designer for Nickelodeon's *Teenage Mutant Ninja Turtles*. Developing a successful manga series in the birthplace of manga had earned him respect in the US comics industry. While Smith was still at Nickelodeon, Marvel Comics asked him to create *All-New Ghost Rider*, a sequel to one of Marvel's biggest-selling titles.

"I wasn't so much wowed by the [style of] manga as I was by its incredible abundance of ordinary, lifelike, slice-of-life scenarios and characters."[40]

—Felipe Smith, American mangaka

These and other international artists reflect the wide cultural reach of what was once a strictly "made in Japan" art tradition. Since 2007 manga artists from abroad have even had their own prestigious International Manga Award. The winners have come from China, Thailand, Belgium, Colombia, Spain, and Mongolia. American writer Joe Kelly and artist J.M. Ken Niimura won in 2011 for *I Kill Giants*, the story of a geeky young misfit with a rich imagination. Established by Japan's Ministry of Foreign Affairs, the International Manga Award is a symbolic recognition that manga and its younger sister anime have become a global art.

$\mathcal{S}$OURCE NOTES

Introduction: A Weird and Wonderful World

1. Roger Ebert, "Japanese Animation Unleashes the Mind," Roger Ebert's Journal, October 7, 1999. www.rogerebert.com.

Chapter One: Stories in Pictures

2. Quoted in Rowan Hooper, "My Seminal Link with Manga God Osamu Tezua," *Japan Times* (Tokyo), September 9, 2012. www.japantimes.co.jp.
3. Quoted in Northrop Davis, *Manga and Anime Go to Hollywood*. New York: Bloomsbury, 2016, pp. 151–52.
4. Quoted in Ryan Holmberg, "Tezuka Osamu and American Comics," *Comics Journal*, July 16, 2012. www.tcj.com.
5. Quoted in Minoru Matsutani, "Manga: Heart of Pop Culture," *Japan Times* (Tokyo), May 26, 2009. www.japantimes.co.jp.
6. Quoted in Planet Genius, "The Godmother of Manga Sex." http://planetgeniusmagazine.com.
7. Quoted in Nicholas Kristof, "In Japan, Brutal Comics for Women," *New York Times*, November 5, 1995. www.nytimes.com.

Chapter Two: Major Manga and Anime Artists

8. Quoted in Joseph Luster, "Miyazaki Blames Otaku Animators for Anime's Decline," *Otaku Magazine USA*, January 31, 2014. www.otakuusamagazine.com.
9. Quoted in Selina Cheng, "'An Insult to Life Itself': Hayao Miyazaki Critiques an Animation Made by Artificial Intelligence," Quartz, December 10, 2016. https://qz.com.
10. Quoted in Nausicaa.net, "Hayao Miyazaki." www.nausicaa.net.
11. Quoted in Zach Logan, "One Piece to Celebrate 20th Anniversary in Weekly Shonen Jump," One Piece Podcast, November 29, 2016. www.onepiecepodcast.com.

12. Quoted in Brian Ashcraft, "The *One Piece* Manga Is 80 Percent Finished, Says Eiichiro Oda," *Kotaku* (blog), July 23, 2018. https://kotaku.com.

13. Jordan Richards, "Silver Spoon Vol. 1 Review," Adventures in Poor Taste, July 13, 2018. www.adventuresinpoortaste.com.

14. Maddy Myers, "What We Still Love About *Cowboy Bebop*, 20 Years Later," *Kotaku* (blog), May 30, 2018. https://kotaku.com.

15. Quoted in A.O. Scott, "Satoshi Kon, Anime Filmmaker, Dies at 46," *New York Times,* August 26, 2010. www.nytimes.com.

16. Manohla Dargis, "In a Crowded Anime Dreamscape, a Mysterious Pixie," *New York Times*, May 25, 2007. http://movies2.nytimes.com.

17. Quoted in Aaron Houghton, "Satoshi Kon's Last Words," Viddy Well, October 23, 2017. www.viddy-well.com.

Chapter Three: The Scene in Japan

18. Quoted in That Japanese Man Yuta, "What Anime Do Japanese People Like?," YouTube, September 18, 2016. www.youtube.com/watch?v=51kkZXYuAb8.

19. 5Cats, March 29, 2014, comment on MyAnimeList, "I Love Love Live and Idolmasters," 2014. https://myanimelist.net.

20. Roland Kelts, *Japanamerica: How Japanese Pop Culture Has Invaded the U.S.* New York: Palgrave Macmillan, 2007, p. 155.

21. 4750G, October 16, 2011, comment on Anime News Network, "Shounen Fighting Series: Why Do People Like Them?," 2011. www.animenewsnetwork.com.

22. Megan R, "The Josei Renaissance," Anime Feminist, April 26, 2017. www.animefeminist.com.

23. Archaeon, November 22, 2008, comment on MyAnimeList, "Saint Oniisan," 2008. https://myanimelist.net.

24. Josh Piedra, "Bakuman Review," Outer Haven, 2015. www.theouterhaven.net.

25. Emily Schendl, "Japanese Anime and Manga and Copyright Reform," *Washington University Global Studies Law Review*, 2016. https://openscholarship.wustl.edu.
26. Quoted in Jeff Blagdon, "Comiket: Shopping for Underground Manga at the World's Biggest Comic Book Event," Verge, August 21, 2012. www.theverge.com.

Chapter Four: Manga and Anime Storm the Planet

27. AniMatsuri, December 14, 2015, comment on Crunchyroll, "Do You Love Crunchyroll?," 2014. www.crunchyroll.com.
28. Protonstorm, "Why I Like Manga More than Western Comics," AniTAY, September 14, 2015. https://anitay.kinja.com.
29. Nicole Clark, "'Avatar: The Last Airbender' Is Still One of the Greatest Shows of All Time," *Vice*, July 20, 2018. www.vice.com.
30. Quoted in Brian Barrett, "Want a Look at Netflix's Future? Follow the Anime," *Wired*, August 2, 2017. www.wired.com.
31. Anime-Planet, "Magi." www.anime-planet.com.
32. Quoted in Hareth al Bustani, "Anime Draws a Crowd in UAE," *National* (Abu Dhabi, United Arab Emirates), November 27, 2016. www.thenational.ae.
33. Quoted in Jean-Yves Katelan, "How Manga Conquered the World," CNRS News, January 24, 2018. https://news.cnrs.fr.
34. Quoted in Jeffrey Hays, "Manga Outside of Japan," Facts and Details, 2013. http://factsanddetails.com.
35. Quoted in Screendriver, "Tales of Wedding Rings VR," Vimeo, 2019. https://vimeo.com.
36. Paula Llanguas, August 13, 2017, comment on Quora, "Why Do You Love Anime?," 2017. www.quora.com.
37. Tsuyuki, "Anime Editorial: The Bliss of Escapism," *Anime Corps* (blog), April 21, 2017. https://animewithsky.wordpress.com.
38. Lilililihhhgf, December 10, 2017, comment on "PaigeeWorld—Art Community," App Store, 2017. https://itunes.apple.com.

39. Lauren Orsini, "Why Netflix Making More Anime May Not Be a Good Thing for Fans," *Forbes*, February 1, 2018. www .forbes.com.

40. Quoted in Tom Pinchuk, "Inside the Manga Industry with Felipe Smith, American Mangaka," Anime News Network, January 19, 2018. www.animenewsnetwork.com.

Books

Hirohiko Araki, *Manga in Theory and Practice*. San Francisco: VIZ Media, 2017.

Toshio Ban, *The Osamu Tezuka Story: A Life in Manga and Anime*. Southbridge, MA: Stonebridge, 2016.

Paul Gravett, *Mangasia: The Definitive Guide to Japanese Comics*. High Holborn, United Kingdom: Thames and Hudson, 2017.

Roland Kelts, *Japanamerica: How Japanese Pop Culture Has Invaded the US*. New York: St. Martin's, 2007.

Frederik Schodt, *Manga! Manga! The World of Japanese Comics*. Tokyo: Kodansha, 2013.

Chris Stuckmann, *Anime Impact: The Movies and Shows That Changed the World of Japanese Animation*. Coral Gables, FL: Mango, 2018.

Internet Sources

Jonah Asher and Yoko Sola, "The Manga Phenomenon," *WIPO Magazine*, September 2011. www.wipo.int.

Jean-Marie Bouissou, "Why Has Manga Become a Global Cultural Product?," *Eurozine*, October 27, 2008. www.eurozine.com.

Kinko Ito, "The *Manga* Culture in Japan," *Japan Studies Review*, 2000. https://asian.fiu.edu.

Japanese Gallery, "History of Japanese *Manga* Comics: The Beginning of *Manga*." www.japanesegallery.co.uk.

Jean-Yves Katelan, "How Manga Conquered the World," *CNRS News*, January 24, 2018. https://news.cnrs.fr.

Minoru Matsutani, "'Manga': Heart of Pop Culture," *Japan Times* (Tokyo), May 26, 2009. www.japantimes.co.jp.

Widewalls, "A Short History of Japanese Manga." www.wide walls.ch.

Websites

AnimeNation (www.animenation.net). A big news site with podcasts, contests, blogs, reviews, and trailers of upcoming anime.

Anime News Network (www.animenewsnetwork.com). This site offers a wealth of information on the industry, as well as an encyclopedia to explain the most obscure terms, techniques, and tropes.

Anime-Planet (www.anime-planet.com). This site is for hardcore fans, with articles, reviews, announcements, online manga chapters, and streaming of forty-five thousand anime episodes.

Crunchyroll (www.crunchyroll.com). This is the leading online anime subscription site, releasing new episodes as they appear in Japan and also offering complete series when they finish. Some content is free.

MyAnimeList (https://myanimelist.net). A site for the latest news on anime and manga projects, also offering community forums and blogs.

INDEX

Picture Credits

Cover: Nyuuness/Shutterstock.com

7: Kyodo News/Newscom
12: Pictures from History/Newscom
15: Serie televise japonaise (manga) Astro Boy, 2003/Bridgeman Images
22: Handout/MTC/Newscom
26: Disney Enterprises/Album/Newscom
30: ReferencePoint Press
34: Photofest Images
40: lydiarei/Shutterstock.com
46: jeagun lee/Shutterstock.com
49: Mahathir Mohd Yasin/Shutterstock.com
54: Album/Newscom
57: Philippe Lissac/GODONG/picture-alliance/Godong/Newscom
63: Pen huang gx/Imaginechina

Tom Streissguth has written more than one hundred books of history, biography, current events, and art history for the school and library market. He has worked as an editor, teacher, journalist, and musician and is collecting the works of famous American journalists. He currently shares time between homes in Minnesota and Thailand.